The "Mary Kay Lady"

WHO ARE THESE REMARKABLE CREATURES???

YOU BETTER FIND OUT WHAT THEY ARE THINKING AND WHY!

It's all about
" Keeping Up with and *Supporting Our Ladies"*

Ladies, help us to understand !

What does a man do these days? Ladies are not behaving as they once did. What do they want from us?

Mary Kay Cosmetics is our example, but it applies to any and all her pursuits.

What do we, as men, have to do with Mary Kay or any other profession they desire?

Ladies, someone had to write this and tell your story……..I hope I did you justice.

Told by a Consultants' Proud Husband
August 2011
Damonboyett@yahoo.com
Copyright c 2011 by Damon Boyett

Preface:

I don't work for Mary Kay and haven't written this for their benefit.

This is written solely for the benefit and enlightenment of the husbands and soul mates of the many Mary Kay consultants throughout the world as well as any ladies contemplating becoming a self employed business person.

<u>I would ask the ladies to forgive me for assuming to know your feelings and wishes. You are certainly invited to unload on me but I hope I have done justice to your feelings. I dearly love you and admire you. Guys, don't make assumptions on me. I am still on our side but some of you just need to wake up before you walk into walls and wonder what happened.</u>

This is not meant to explain the policies or procedures of Mary Kay or any other company. It is meant only to outline what husbands and soul mates might expect since this information is so important to our ladies and their careers. It is now just as important to the guys and their relationships for the future.

It also reflects the authors' passion and respect for the "fairer sex". As such, this book is really meant for any husband/soul mate with a working wife/partner. You know, the "Weaker Sex"!

The "Weaker Sex"! Give me a break! Think about it. You haven't really believed that in years. If you have, you are either preoccupied completely with yourself or been a guest on another planet.

What I am about to impart to you is not affected by income bracket, social status, or occupation. However it is important enough in your life to either cement your relationship or insure that you are going to lose her.......YOUR CHOICE, TAKE IT SERIOUSLY OR NOT.......

Chapter One

Since the onset of the apple (fruit, not the computer) there has been this special and splendid creature we call woman. Most everyone would agree, upon thought, that they are special.

This book is for the men who consider their choice of mates to be good, not a mistake. If you think you made a mistake, this might even be good for you and provide a means of keeping her busy and away from you. If that is the case, she is probably heading in that direction anyway. (staying away from you) Good grief, it might even repair what has been going wrong.

Ah yes! **Ladies,** God bless them, are born into this male dominated macho world expected to care for their husbands and/or mates in all manner of luxury. From being trained by their mothers at childhood, to refining their cooking and household skills through high school, they learn how to serve and make others happy. Through the ages and even today, society, including women, have so underestimated the talents and abilities of this gender. In no small part we men have sold them short, especially when challenges outside the household are concerned. Once upon a time women supported their men by saying "yes" to everything he said or wanted and obeyed his every wish. I saw it in my family as well as relatives.

Wonderful women, sweet as can be and devoted to killing themselves as mothers and wives. Only women could get it all done and obey everyone's wishes. They had no career themselves as that was out of the question. They were needed at home. Don't even think about it.

We, of course, as their mates, have always expected them to *stretch* themselves and take on a few more *untrained* and sometimes *unexpected* demands. Those, of course, range from pleasing us in the manner we desire, as we *spring on them with our expectations,* to their washing, ironing, shopping, sewing and preparing our choice of meals (on time, of course).

We must also have our neck rubs and nightly sympathy sessions to release our tensions from our hard day at the office or plant. She must be attentive as we explain all the ills that have befallen us during our long day of earning that fat paycheck that we earn to supply us with our bass boats and restored cars. In some cases we give her an allowance if she can assure us she can responsibly handle it. Oh yea, if there is any money left over we will try to arrange to give her enough for that purse or pair of shoes she might need. However with all her expected duties, where would she get the time to wear new things? Why would she need more shoes? We don't take her anywhere, so where is the need anyway? Oh yea, I guess she could wear them to visit her mother and brag a bit.

As if that's not enough, she bears the expectation of giving birth to our children while she uses her spare time to keep our immaculate house, the refrigerator full, pets groomed, garden weeded and lawn watered. You know, it just occurred to me that the ladies on ranches and farms also have a bunch of animals to care for in addition to everything else mentioned above. Wow! There is a bunch of ladies living outside of the cities, uh?

All well, don't feel sorry for her as this only goes on for 18 to 20 years, then the kids leave home and she can relax. After all, she certainly has her life and responsibilities laid out before her. It's not as though she doesn't have everything. She has it all, uh guys.

Chapter Two

At some point in time IT arrives. We, as men, are forced to give of ourselves in a very unfair manner. As our women perform these routine tasks, they sometimes get sick. They, like any machine will go down occasionally. Let's face it fellows, it's really the luck of the draw. Did you inspect those teeth closely as your daddy told you? Did you get a good one or is yours' breaking down once in a while? After all, it's been proven that plenty of women can have a baby in the field, put it in their backpack and continue to pick the crops. They did it in ancient times.

But, we didn't all get one of those. It seems ours may need the doctor and hospital these days to give birth.

Now we, as men, again have trouble cast upon us. We must now care for the children and ourselves at home. We must do some laundry (ha ha, buy more clothes is my answer), all of which increases our burden on time and therefore stresses our golf game. Can't she come home an hour after giving birth? I heard that it's good for her to get back on her feet right away.

As we are *all soon aware*, we male supermen could not survive performing the required work of our beautiful female partners. We couldn't find or buy the organization they possess. We would die before putting up with the pain they go through every day without showing it. The many cycles they possess in their bodies, the emotions they keep within themselves (we hope), the patience they exhibit with every waking minute of their lives could *only* be done by a female.

"What do you mean, cut her some slack, she is eating for two now." "Her hormones are going wild and crazy." "Try and understand", we are told. Her doctor has told you she shouldn't be doing all these duties at home while pregnant. She should take it easy.

"We understand, let us help". We men are more than happy to "step up" and hire a mid wife or maid to help get this done. You must remember our schedule continues, no matter what new problems you ladies are having. If we can't afford a mid wife, surely a mother-in-law can step up.

By this time you have probably hidden all the mirrors in the house as you read this. Trouble looking at yourself, are you? Look at her and what she is going through. We can really be disgusting.

Look at that tender and loving creature who is and has been doing everything she can to please us and still manages to contend with the daily demands set upon her. As many of us know, having been thrust into being a substitute mother and household chief for a day or week, we are neither capable or willing to pull it off. "How does she do it?" we ask silently.

It is not possible to get all this done in a day. It gives us wonder as we happen to remember that she does all this while in pain or while pregnant <u>and</u> in pain. She also does it with those multiple, tiny, sweet, adorable and minding children hanging on her at the same time. Oh yea, I forgot. We might have put her through this before. Who are these creatures, these women? Are they even human? It sure didn't seem possible the last time I had to try and step in their shoes.

"These machines" perform these loving duties all their life. For some, it's *out of love* for husband and family. For others, it's what *they have to do*, as it's expected of them by everyone, family and friends. It is a wonder they don't explode every hour, on the hour. Some do, you say?.........and we wonder why?

Do we ever try to thank them? Do we show them how appreciated they are? Well, after all, we are rather busy and need them to get all these things done. Our mother did it, didn't she? I don't remember hearing her complain.

Let's see, I know I must have told her how much I appreciate what she does. Didn't I?
Seems I did. Oh well, she always seem to forget it when I do and claims I never did.
I think she knows it. I'm sure she does.

But, it seems once in a while our ladies feel the need to try and enlighten us on their feelings...............Oh lord, another one of those sessions coming our way..........I told you, sometimes they forget how we showed them we appreciate them. I think the last time was last year, taking all of them camping. Yea, I fished all day on the boat and she relaxed and played with the kids at the campsite. "Yea, that was it". After all, I got her away from the house and all that work. She and the kids seemed to have fun, running (well, maybe it was chasing) I sure rested a bunch; even slept some too.

Chapter Three

"Oh," we men say, "if all this is too much for you, why don't *you* get a job and that will take your mind off the kids and the pressures of home life. It might even help the lack of *adult* contact you are always carrying on about." <u>Shame on you mister when you didn't notice that she started talking in the language of a four-year-old.</u> You probably thought she fell that day and broke something in her brain.

This especially gives birth to the time in her life where she discovers "self fulfillment". Why isn't she happy? Now wait a minute! She was foretold by her mother and all of society that having a family and beautiful children would be the pinnacle of life. So what is wrong?

She doesn't know what's wrong either. She just knows something is not as it should be. She feels that she is not herself and the more she thinks about it, the worse it seems……….Oh my, here comes trouble ………..She should not be feeling this way.

Now gentlemen, it's time to put this entire situation into perspective and get down to the point of this entire book. She is no different than us. She has a need for "self worth" just as we do.

We deal with it without realizing it through our chosen work, job and hobbies. Sometimes our hobbies may only be meeting the guys at the club or local bar. She can't do that, she has home responsibilities with kids, house, yard, washing, and meals.

We work all day and go to our hobbies after work. She worked all day and has *duties galore* the rest of the night. No time for her to play. You ever thought about it this way?
Well, it seems the kids and home are not doing their job in satisfying this gal. Isn't that a wonder. Too many of these remarkable creatures don't get any support or more importantly, recognition from their mates and families. They are begging to be appreciated for what they are and what they do.

Your lady is hungry to be treated as a lady, respected and given thanks for her lifetime of commitment and sacrifices to others. She never dresses up during the day. Why should she?

The kids won't notice.   Neither will you most of the time. To be recognized for this would be no less than she deserves.

<u>Why are so many women raising a family alone as a one-parent family?</u>

Easy answer:

In many cases, it's only because they became *fed up* with <u>GETTING NO RETURN ON THEIR INVESTMENT.</u>

In modern times our ladies have been inspired by various motivations to take a good look at themselves and reevaluate their lives as well as their self worth.

Chapter Four

In the past, the rewards for all her efforts, long hours of running a household and raising those children, were enough.

In this day and age of female CEO's and female astronauts, she feels no longer willing to take the "second seat" but rather wants to be in the "pilot" seat. She feels, somehow, she could balance the responsibilities of being a wife and mother with the pursuit of a successful career. Once that inner thought gives birth, anything posing to stop this pursuit will be negated. She won't allow it. Her ambition eats at her and she is only asking that her love ones "get on board" and support her efforts toward that goal.

If, for some reason, her family rejects or slows her down by not supporting her, trouble is sure to follow. Marriages have fallen here, as this trouble can easily take the form of divorce or separation, especially if she has tasted success. This splendid creature, able to rise to new heights in her life, wants nothing to get in her way. She only wants that needed support and strongly prays that it will come from her family. She expects it and why not? Has she not spent her entire life supporting us and in many more ways than she is asking for in return?

In most cases her quest will be a new venture for her and she feels frightened and unsure of the outcome as she travels through these unknown waters. But, as sure as the sun will rise tomorrow morning, she is just as determined to try. As with many of us, these feelings haunt us all as we live our lives wading through various career changes. Remember these times, guys? Who was it encouraging us and assuring us that we could make it? Who did we lean on? *Now she needs us!*

Actually we, as their mates, have it quite easy in supporting them. Our contribution doesn't take more than a little effort. We aren't called on to perform miracles, as our ladies are. We have no physical effort to expend as they do and no pain to endure.

Chapter Five

Mary Kay came about in my personal life as my beautiful lady was already using their products. She had purchased her products from one of the organizations' consultants as everyone does. Her consultant was going out of business as she was told by her husband that she would no longer work and would only stay home and work for him. It was in her make up to abide by his wishes and she quit representing Mary Kay.

It was at that point my wife investigated being able to buy her personal cosmetics on a wholesale basis as a result of becoming a Mary Kay Consultant. She spoke with a director and gathered the details to present to me.

You must, at this point, understand my background. I have enjoyed a successful career and possess a varied business background. I have owned my own businesses, served as a top executive for corporate America, as well as having either participated or investigated in about every business opportunity known to man. I learned the ins and outs of schemes. Some of these have made money, some have lost. I have been in sales for many years, both as a salesman and sales manager. I was an auto mechanic and machinist before serving in the U.S. Army. Talk about life changing............He sure helps me to understand what she is going through.

On one rainy Sunday morning I am presented with this seemingly beautiful opportunity. My wife informs me she can buy her cosmetics wholesale and doesn't have to do anything else to maintain this ability. She gave me the literature and asks me to look it over. I deeply researched this for her to find the "catches". After all, wouldn't I be the hero, finding all the "hidden scams" in this opportunity she has become enthused with. In the end I only pointed out each requirement to her only to find that she had already been told of them. Her consultant had offered to show her how a career with Mary Kay could work for her but was told by my wife that she wasn't interested. My wife is a full time nurse and most satisfied. Well, at least at that time.

I must stop here and explain that my beautiful wife has the smile of an angel. She is quite shy but is quite friendly with everyone she gets to know. In fact, all who know her deeply love her. She, however, would not initiate a conversation with any stranger. She would even ask me to compose and send her emails to her family members and friends. She was so shy on the computer, in fact, scared to death of it.

Knowing this, it did not concern me as she was not going to sell this product, only use it.

So I gave my certified stamp of approval on the proposal. After all, it was going to save me money in the long run, not cost me. She would be required to become a consultant for a fee but wouldn't be burdened with the sales aspect.

She then signed an agreement as a consultant with Mary Kay and readied her first personal order. The consultant, whom she had signed with, who happened to be a Director with Mary Kay called her and invited her to attend a weekly meeting of her team, so that my wife could assure herself that her decision to forgo Mary Kay as a career, was indeed the correct choice.
I encouraged her to attend, mainly to eliminate any future questions or doubts on the subject.

What the heck, it couldn't hurt……

Chapter Six

My wife returned from that meeting with a strange look on her face. I sensed a change in this woman before me. An invisible fire had ignited and was burning somewhere within her. Although unsure of this thing call sales, she was more excited about this than when she first laid eyes on me. (we know that's impossible)

I sat there listening to this explosion of enthusiasm and couldn't help but love her that much more. God, she was beautiful, sitting there, standing there, sitting there (excited) with this glow about her. She was so enthused, but yet seemed skeptical about her abilities to sell and wondered what I thought of the possibilities. Since I had experienced a successful sales career as well as having hired and seen so many failed salespeople over the years, she was anxious to get my opinion. (Now that alone told me that I had been doing something right, that she was even asking my opinion)

Having been surprised a number of times throughout my career by the performance of others, I, (who would have lost a tremendous amount of money betting on whether others could or could not sell), looked dead into her eyes and spoke.

Guys, at this point, we, as their mates, hold our future in our mouths. We, <u>at that instant,</u> have the power to make or destroy a career and even possibly our marriage/relationship with what dribbles next out of our mouths. All I could think of was that we teach our children and students to "think before they speak". I decided to take my own advice. You think I was going to tell her she couldn't do it? Yea right…..

I responded, "Honey, I think you could be a winner at anything you made your mind up to do."
"You are that good and have proven it time after time throughout your life." "I think you are a remarkable woman and who knows what lurks inside you." <u>That,</u> my friends, got me the biggest hug I have ever had. I discovered her mind was made up before the question was asks. (imagine that) But I didn't say anything more as I had just been declared the "cure for cancer".

I might also address the residual effect of what I said. Upon finishing my answer, I could have achieved several things. I could have been crowned a king, upgraded myself to a suite, bought myself any number of new tools for my woodshop or any number of wonderful things that I will leave you to imagine.

Fact:

Time after time, **desire continues to overcome talent**.

We see it in athletics all the time. It's called "upsets".

<u>After all, who are we to tell someone they can't do something.</u>

Chapter Seven

Well, as with fireworks, her fuse was lit and she took off like a rocket, calling friends and co-workers, talking with other ladies, many who were strangers and she achieved instant success. My shy, lovable partner suddenly talked to everyone and was so cute doing it. As soon as she was alone she would breathe deep and give me that "I did it" smile. Shopping in stores and paying the rent was no longer a quiet affair. High fives were given and have since. It will never end. She sells anyone and everyone she meets and has a ball doing it. She loves her product and herself. She hands out those cards everywhere. She talks them into having some type of party to have fun and sell her products.

She has never lost an inch in her enthusiasm and grows daily in her business. She sometimes, like all of us, has her down times where things go bad and sales are slow. Those are the times where she needs to hear from us. She doesn't need to be informed of how bad the economic times are right now, rather how good things are. She needs to be encouraged, not discouraged. She is looking to be supported and needs it. She has discovered that thing called <u>sales</u> was a distant embryo within her which has been fertilized and is growing in leaps and bounds. Her moods, ups and downs, have disappeared and she is happy each and every day. She dresses to the nines (classy for you non-Southern readers) each day and will not be seen without being "put together". She reeks of pride.

Please remember:

It is Attitude that brings success; it is also Attitude that kills it!

Her attitude is fed by you, her mate! So, I am assuming you are beginning to see where your part in this might be. Remember don't make her start wondering whether she needs a mate or not. She is on fire and needs support, not an attitude coming from her guy.

This ride with her is going to eat time, maybe formerly your time with your lady and the family. Understanding on your part is needed badly. Do yourself a favor. Give her a phone, her phone with a new number. Make sure she has a computer. They are tax deductible. She possibly needs your assistance with $$ starting out. She must reinvest in her business in order to build it. She must buy back most of what she sells at first as well as order new product to build her inventory. She also needs an office in the home, but hopefully not in the living room where the family resides. My wife and I make appointments with one another in the planner. It does work for things such as dinners, lunches, etc. It keeps her from booking parties and functions on *our* time. This makes a big difference.

Chapter Eight

Many husbands and mates don't have a sales or marketing background. But they do have a sense of what is right and wrong. They can still help and reinforce her efforts. If the closet is full of inventory and sales are not happening, they have the sense to know it's not suppose to be that way. The bank account gets empty and help is needed.

Your ladies emotional and mental status at any time is paramount. People can do remarkable things when encouraged and supported. <u>It's so much easier to climb when someone helps you hold the rope.</u>

I started to affect my support by reading her manual that she brought home. I read it page by page. She loved the amount of interest I showed (I gave her <u>no</u> negative feedback)

All of a sudden she is signing up for the offered computer web site for herself, sending and receiving emails from customers and the company. She is researching web sites, cosmetic techniques, all on the internet. She is designing forms and handouts for customers. She is designing packages for her prospects and customers as well as parties she is planning and holding. She became an organizing fool. I just stood back and marveled. At times she asks for me to help with form design on the computer. I was just lending my expertise when requested. That is very important. I did not want to push myself on her. If she had a problem, I would offer my help. I discovered that showing her one time on the computer was all that was necessary. Wow, it was the first time she had responded like that, being shown one time and running with it from there.

One week she was crippled on the computer, next week was its master. I guess you can tell I am pretty proud of her.

The fear was gone. "Please show me how", she formerly asked. The next night she was off on her own, only to proudly show me her completed project. If I think of an easier or better way I will point it out to her only if the timing seems right. You guys know what I mean. (She now thinks I am a genius on the computer, ha ha) I just relate that there is alternate ways of doing things on the computer. Weigh them out and choose which one you like best. That way I am not dictating to her. I now get asks to "proof read" her advertising and forms. <u>It's important to her, so it's important to me.</u> Here is where you lay down what you are doing and give all your attention to her.

Chapter Nine

As with any sales job, people will disappoint
occasionally. Someone will not show up.
Someone may lie to you. Someone may be late.
Someone will not show or have the decency to
call you and let you know. When this happens
to our lady, we must step up and encourage
them. They have been let down. They think
they have done something wrong, maybe when
inviting them.

Point out to her that it is what we do when
disappointed or let down, that makes us
successful or not. Not letting others "spoil" our
day but rather finding someone else to lift it, is
the answer. "Find someone else and
immediately sell them something", is always the
best cure. My lady has done it time and again
and finds it lifts her to new heights. Believe me,
it has all paid dividends. Don't let me kid you;
the dividends have come my way, if no other
way than in the form of a happy wife. She holds
meetings and parties and always brings the
happiness home. After a while she started
bringing home all manner of awards and
goodies for the work she has done.   That all
brings happiness and elevates her self esteem.

<u>Meetings and parties</u>: Be ready for those at your house on weeknights and sometimes weekends. They are events she needs in her business and she sells and exposes a lot of product at these functions. Oh mercy, trouble started for me when that occurred. " I am going to be put out of my house tonight for hours. " What about my favorite movie or TV program?" " Where am I to go?" I did not like it. Our home was not set up to function this way. I even heard of one husband who sat right in the middle of the living room watching TV while his wife conducted a party with six ladies sitting all around him. What a jerk! He really cares about helping his wife be successful.   I might inform you, happily, that she kicked him out of the house a short time ago and is growing her business quite well now without a mate.

As for me, I worked it out by going to the bedroom, watching TV or reading for that 2-2 ½ hours. Not bad after all. Especially when she opens the door with that big grin on her face saying that it was a great party and "thank you" for allowing it to happen. She has sold a lot of product and booked more future parties. Believe me, I get the rewards.   (Most of the parties, however, are not in your home but the customer's.)

GET THIS! Pay Attention! You won't believe this one……..

I actually asked my wife "what can I do to help you"? As most of the guys know, I must have a screw loose to ask such a thing. (equivalent to offering my soul on a chopping block)

Her Answer: "Nothing baby, you are already doing it."

I cook many nights for us. I sometime drive her to different places she needs to deliver product, present shows and attend meetings. We at least get to "be together" for those moments. I then pick her up and help her bring home those rewards she earned.

Chapter Ten

I saved to buy her a new personal computer, just for her. (another means of supporting her and the wonderful progress she is making.)

She has become so creative just from enthusiasm. I support her in expressing my pride in her and for her many accomplishments. I have attended meetings to see her receive awards and take photos for our album. I stop what I am doing when she approaches. I look her in the eye when she is talking about her adventures. Being a "closet chef", I even cook a few things for her parties. Yea, I know, but I make the time. They really are worth it, fellows. When she has a special typing project on the computer I will offer to type it for her as she is still "hunting and pecking", but never complains.

She has really developed a strong sense of achievement and will always carry that with her, no matter how far she ever goes with the company. I have never seen such goal setting and maintaining. She has achieved her goals much earlier than planned and has constantly readjusted them. She is asked to attend meetings once a week. She can't wait for them and loves them. I adjust my schedule if necessary, to make sure she can go.

She opened her own bank account and operates her business within those funds. When I am able, out of the family account, I will contribute something special as a surprise.
That is usually in the form of buying her a larger display case or additional samples she has wanted or needed, but couldn't yet afford. Of course, I have no idea of what she needs but will give her the funds to get them as I hear of her needing them, when possible. Anything I can do to support her efforts, I will do. Our precious ladies are special and deserve all we can do for them. Each time a major accomplishment is completed, I send flowers if the bank account allows.

Her self esteem has risen to new heights and has become a story that should be told.

So shall yours, if she gets your support. This is so important to her. Would you want to live with the one that fails because of getting no support? I don't know where she will go with this but I know how happy she is now and how proud she is of herself. She is so confident in her life now. What have I done? I have tried to give her the time to reach her goals <u>without the guilt</u> for having to do what was necessary.

After every meeting, I make it a point to ask how it went and how many dollars were sold. Any new prospects (consultants) developed? Any new customers sold? How many new bookings? I just express genuine interest. "How did it go?" just doesn't cut it. It is not sincere and it shows........See, I talk in her Mary Kay language. We talk, I listen.....

My wife and I keep a common planner in additional to our own. Normally Saturday and Sunday are mine with her. Saturday mostly is questionable during the day. That's OK as I am usually busy working in my woodshop or playing golf. We may do nothing, but she is all mine and I want to make sure it's worth taking the time with me and not wishing she could work on Mary Kay.

Her appointments are on the common planner so neither of us books over the other.

She has surprised me in so many ways. I am so fascinated by the organizational skills that these ladies develop. My wife and I are basically neat people. Neither of us will put up with messes being left out without being put away. With her inventory and materials, I expected some trouble between us. Wow, she stepped out ahead of that one. Not a thing out of place in that office (bedroom, just for her office), building shelves, cabinets painted after being found in garage sales.

She finds other women selling business opportunities, IE: Avon, Princess, scrapbooking, candles, soaps, etc. "I'll buy your product and throw you a party, you book a party for me and buy mine." It works so great. She even recruits them as consultants on her team if they are good. She just signed one of them last week. "SMART LADY, uh?"

She has informed me recently that she is working hard toward winning her first car with Mary Kay. Guys, I really think this lady will make it. But if she doesn't, look what she has become.

Prologue:

I sincerely hope in some manner or capacity that I have awakened someone and given them the opportunity to reflect on their own lives. It's just that I have seen and talked with so many women across the United States and abroad, heard the problems and complaints about their husbands/mates. I really don't understand how this problem continues. If you don't want to support your ladies, you probably won't have long to worry about it. These ladies are one incident away from leaving you and finding someone who will. Many have already done it all alone. Most don't want to, but are really tired of searching for someone who will be honest with them and willing to commit to a real life. It's a different world out there now, guys. **They are not asking for much**. I hear it over and over.

Good luck ladies!

I again invite any and all comments from you. I certainly love any suggestions for content and comment. As times get tougher, so does the pressures on relationships. It's a subject dear to us all and I am proud to address it. Someone needs to.......

This material was taken from a portion of my new book currently underway but as yet untitled.

In the mist of writing it, I was moved to write this short story about the self employed ladies and the changing of their lives.   I suddenly discovered that I had already written about them in my new book and extracted ideas from there to create this book.

Watch for it and I hope you will enjoy it and in some way benefit from it. It is also about those unique and wonderful creatures and the messages they are sending to those who are listening.

I hope you will visit me when my web site is finished.

MY HAT IS OFF TO ALL YOU LADIES, YOU ARE SO VERY SPECIAL.........

Damon Boyett
Damonboyett@yahoo.com
August 2011

DAMON BOYETT has enjoyed a colorful career since being born and raised in Texas. At the age of 13, he was already working and driving. He worked at many jobs while attending school. After returning from Europe, having served in 13 different countries with the US Army Intelligence Service, he eventually found his new career in sales. Being transferred around the United States with his family, he found his love in the corporate world, selling and managing people. He now embarks on a new career as an author. He loves writing and is busy on his first full non-fiction book in helping relationships. His experience has touched him deeply in helping others to see where they are and where they can go in their lives. He lives with his beautiful wife in Northern California.